CW01429770

The election of a pope

by
Mgr Charles Burns OBE

All booklets are published thanks to the
generous support of the members of the
Catholic Truth Society

CATHOLIC TRUTH SOCIETY
PUBLISHERS TO THE HOLY SEE

Contents

Foreword

The election of a pope is one of the most interesting and indeed most important events to occur in the world.

The Pope is not only the visible head of the Roman Catholic Church but also undoubtedly the most widely heard and, it is to be hoped, heeded spiritual voice in the world.

Thus, the outcome of a papal election is of interest not only to Catholics but to all Christians and indeed to people of every faith and of none. It is also of great interest to political leaders, as is evidenced by the more than 160 countries which maintain diplomatic relations with the Holy See.

Perhaps no one is better equipped to explain the method and history of such elections than Mgr Charles Burns, who has devoted most of his priestly life to dedicated work in the Vatican Secret Archives, a service from which he retired after 35 years. In 1998 he received the OBE from the Queen, and is now ecclesiastical advisor to the British Embassy to the Holy See. He teaches at the Papal Ecclesiastical Academy.

Mgr Burns has prepared a brief but most informative and intensely interesting study of how a man is chosen to lead the flock of Christ and to fill the shoes of the Fisherman.

✠ *John Patrick Cardinal Foley*

The election of a pope

It falls to the Cardinal Camerlengo, or Chamberlain of the Holy Roman Church, to announce officially the death of the Pope and thereby declare the Holy See to be vacant. The Church enters into that period of mourning and expectancy which separates pontificates. For several weeks the eyes of the world will be focused on the Vatican. Why? Who is the Pope that his death and the election of a successor should attract such widespread attention?

The Pope

In the Vatican's official handbook the reigning pope is described by many titles: Bishop of Rome, Vicar of Jesus Christ, Successor of St Peter Prince of the Apostles, Supreme Pontiff of the Universal Church, Patriarch of the West, Primate of Italy, Archbishop and Metropolitan of the Roman Province, Sovereign of Vatican City State. All these are strictly correct, because they correspond to precise theological, canonical, historical and legal realities, even though nowadays many of them are seldom used explicitly. The list includes one last title: Servant of the Servants of God, which was introduced by St Gregory the Great (590–604) and has been retained by all his successors as particularly expressive of the role of the papacy in the Universal Church.

Strangely, there is one that does not figure on the list: the title 'Pope'! Yet that is probably the most commonly known title of all. The word '*Papa*' meaning 'Pope' comes from the Greek word '*papas*' meaning 'father', or even better in its more endearing form 'papa'. In very early times, it was used to express affectionate veneration for the bishop; it is still used in this way by the Orthodox churches to designate any priest, just as Catholics refer to their priests as 'father' in the Latin Church. In the West from the end of the fourth century it tended to be a specific and distinctive title of the Bishop of Rome, Liberius (352–366) being the first to style himself in this way. In 1073, Pope Gregory VII prohibited its use by any other bishop than the Roman Pontiff.

The popes can trace a continuous line of succession from St Peter (Pope John Paul II is reckoned as the 264th successor), and the papacy, originating in the days of the early Roman Empire, is the longest surviving institution in the world. There is an impressive series of portraits of all the popes on a frieze inside the basilica of St Paul-outside-the-Walls; each mosaic medallion is accompanied by the name of the Pontiff and the exact duration of his pontificate calculated in years, months and days. Only twenty-eight roundels have yet to be filled.

Christ alone is Head of the Church; in communion with her we become limbs of His mystical Body. The Pope, therefore, serves as His vicar or locum tenens on earth and is simply the visible head of the Church. He is the spiritual leader of approximately nine hundred and seventy six million Roman Catholic faithful, who owe him obedience and remain in communion with him, referring to him as their Holy Father, as befits the charge entrusted to him as successor of Peter to feed Christ's lambs and His sheep. Millions outside his flock also look to him for moral guidance and hold him in high respect. His influence is enormous. For these and other reasons the entire world must reckon with the Pope and that explains the interest shown in the papal election.

Sede Vacante

The death of the Pope, be it sudden and unpredicted, or preceded by illness and advanced age, must never throw the Church into crisis, nor, for that matter, would his free resignation from the papacy. The last to abdicate was Pope Celestine V, in 1294; he died two years later. In 1313 he was declared a saint, though this did not deter Dante from ascribing him to hell in the pages of the *Divina Commedia*! There are, however, no canonical procedures for deposing an impaired, mentally deranged, senile, comatose, or, even worse, a manifestly unworthy pope; the papacy is vacated only by his demise or renunciation, no matter how extreme the circumstances and degree of incapacitation.

It has been the duty of the popes to make appropriate laws to provide for any normal eventuality that can arise during a vacancy or interregnum of this unique office, termed in Latin the *sede vacante*. Enacted over the course of many centuries, but recently updated (22 February 1996) and clearly set out by Pope John Paul II in the Apostolic Constitution entitled *Universi Dominici Gregis* and in the *Motu proprio* of Benedict XVI, 11th June 2007, abrogating the provision contained in paragraph 75 of the Apostolic Constitution that made a simple majority of votes sufficient for a valid election in unusual circumstances. These laws entrust restricted interim powers of government to the cardinals; they regulate meticulously the ceremonials and establish the rules, all of which must be faithfully observed in electing the new pope.

Our purpose here is to examine briefly, with only an occasional backward glance at the historical context, this code of legislation from the instant it comes into force with the death or resignation of the pope, until the election of his successor.

The Cardinals

The essential administration of the Church is not brought to a standstill. The Cardinal Camerlengo (appointed to this position by the reigning pontiff personally, or elected to it provisionally, if the post is vacant at the time of his death, by a secret ballot of the cardinal electors), the Cardinal Major Penitentiary (also a personal papal nominee to whose judgment the gravest cases of conscience are submitted for absolution, which must always be available), the Cardinal Vicar of Rome (equal to the vicar general of a diocese) and the Cardinal Archpriest of St Peter's Basilica (who is also Vicar General for Vatican City), all remain in office; whereas the Cardinal Secretary of State, the cardinal prefects of the Congregations and the presidents of the various councils and offices of the Roman Curia cease to exercise their functions. At the Vatican, the Substitute (or second in command) of the Secretariat of State, the Secretary for Relations with States (equivalent of a minister for foreign affairs), and the numerous other Secretaries remain in charge of their respective curial departments. The apostolic nuncios and apostolic delegates continue in office at their posts throughout the world.

The Cardinal Dean convokes the Sacred College of Cardinals, all of whom must obey his summons unless legitimately impeded, and provisionally the government passes to their hands, at least for contingent matters, while all major decisions are deferred until after the election of the new pontiff. Their powers are strictly limited and they cannot tamper with the rules for the papal election, co-opt new cardinals to the College during the interregnum, or take decisions binding on the next pope.

The cardinals already present in Rome, – and hourly, with the arrival of the others from near and far, the number increases, – assemble daily in the Vatican Palace for what are called the General Cardinalitial Congregations, meetings at which all, without exception or limit of age, must take part, unless, as in the exceptional case of the octogenarian non-electors, they prefer not to attend. A tangible sign that the government of the Church is in their hands can be seen in the practice (dating from 1521) of striking commemorative medals and minting coins bearing the heraldic arms of the Cardinal Camerlengo surmounted by the Pavilion – a large ceremonial umbrella, striped alternately in red and yellow silk – in combination with the Keys crossed in saltire, traditionally (from the twelfth century onwards) the emblem representing the temporal power of the Church. Since 1939, there has also been a special sede vacante issue of Vatican City postage stamps displaying the same heraldic device.

Nunc dimittis

Under the direction of the general congregations, the arrangements must be made for the funeral rites of the deceased pope, which are solemnised for nine

The coffin placed before St Peter's.

consecutive days, the *novendiali* of official mourning, in accordance with the rubrics of the *Ordo Exsequiarum Romani Pontificis*, the order of service for the burial of the Roman pontiff. The burial itself should take place between four and six days after death, unless there is some exceptional reason for a postponement, and eventual personal dispositions of the deceased should be respected.

The solemn liturgy is officiated by the Cardinal Dean with poignant sobriety in keeping with the sadness of the occasion. Traditionally the remains of the Pope repose inside a coffin of cypress-wood, encased within a second one of lead with an inscription bearing his name and the dates of the pontificate, which in its turn is contained by a third outer coffin of elm. How strikingly isolated it seems, exposed unadorned on the vast threshold of St Peter's Basilica, in sight of hundreds of thousands of mourners who have flocked into the Square in reverent silence to pay their last respects.

Meantime the Cardinal Camerlengo, who is entrusted with safeguarding the temporal rights and administering the material possessions of the Holy See during the sede vacante, attends personally to the breaking of the 'Fisherman's Ring', the gold signet ring of the popes, with at its centre an engraving of St Peter casting his net from a boat and the name of the reigning pontiff inscribed around the rim. This act is performed in the presence of the other cardinals and is the official sign that all pontifical power is suspended. He must also see to the sealing-off of the private papal apartments with their contents, and to placing other papal properties, such as the Lateran Palace and the summer villa at Castel Gandolfo, under special custody; after the election they will be consigned intact to the new pope.

Preparations for the election

The preparations for the forthcoming election must be put in motion. In practice this is the competence of the Cardinal Camerlengo and three elected cardinal assistants, one from each order of bishops, priests and deacons. Every three days this trio is replaced by others, also chosen by lot, until a new pope is elected. They meet in 'particular congregations' to handle minor matters on a daily basis, deferring any more serious questions to the preparatory 'general congregations' of all the cardinals.

Hitherto finding accommodation for the cardinals and their retinues presented a formidable logistical problem. Not only were the makeshift cells far from comfortable and unhygienic, erected haphazardly here and there in draughty corridors and halls of the Vatican Palace, but they also constituted a major fire risk, being only provisional and constructed of potentially inflammable materials.

It is said that the Colonnade of St Peter's Square was designed by the architect Gian Lorenzo Bernini in the mid seventeenth century, specifically with the idea (which might in fact have been Francesco Borromini's) of incorporating a sufficient number of rooms on top to lodge the Sacred College during an election. Likewise, that the monumental Sacristy with its spacious central rotunda, ideal as an election chamber, and the connecting residence for the canons serving the Basilica were intended by Pope Pius VI, in 1784, as a solution to this recurring problem, to be vacated in favour of the cardinals for the duration of an interregnum.

Recently that matter has finally been resolved. The task of the special commission composed of the Cardinal Camerlengo, the former Cardinal Secretary of State and the former Cardinal President of the Pontifical Commission for Vatican City State, has been greatly simplified by the construction of a purpose-built residence within the Vatican, the *Domus S. Marthae* – 'St Martha's House' – inaugurated by the Pope on 31 May 1996. It comprises one hundred and thirty suites and single rooms to provide adequate and comfortable, but also suitably secluded accommodation, with full facilities and refectory service, for the cardinals and a restricted group of assistants. The hospice is designed to ensure them complete freedom from interference or pressure from the world outside for the duration of the election,

Domus S. Marthae.

which will continue to take place as normally in the Sistine Chapel situated nearby, within the precinct of the Vatican Palace and now suitably adapted to allow the process to proceed in a smooth and orderly manner. Stringent measures will be enforced so that no one may communicate with them as they shuttle back and forth between the hospice and the chamber.

Above all, in one of the general congregations, the cardinals must fix the day and the hour when they will withdraw and enter the conclave. This cannot begin until at least fifteen full days have elapsed since the Holy See was declared vacant in order to allow sufficient time for absent electors to reach the Vatican; but when a maximum of twenty days have passed all those present must proceed to the election.

The conclave and its history

The conclave is a meeting place that can be locked securely. It is a room where discussions can be held in private, without fear of intrusion. The English word is derived from two Latin words, '*cum*', meaning 'with', plus '*clave*', meaning 'a key': a place where those assembled are under lock and key. In the course of time this word, 'conclave' has come to be applied to the place, and to those gathered in it, and to one assembly in particular: the assembly of the cardinals, who have withdrawn themselves apart for the express purpose of electing a new pope. The word was first used in connection with the papal election in a decree of Pope Gregory X, issued in July 1274, at the second General Council of Lyons, which has regulated the procedure since that time. Behind the idea of a papal conclave there is a long and colourful history.

We must go back to the thirteenth century, if we are to understand the reason for the conclave, and see what happened after the death of Pope Clement IV (29 November 1268). He died at Viterbo, a small town to the north of Rome, and the cardinals met there to elect a successor, but failed to reach agreement. Weeks dragged into months, and months lengthened into years, but still the deadlock continued and there was no sign of a new pope being elected. Then the citizens of Viterbo, exasperated with the indifference of the cardinals to the scandal caused by the stalemate, decided to wall up the electors inside the palace, until such time as they fulfilled their obligations with proper seriousness. Stone-masons sealed off the entrance, leaving only a small wicket gate through which food, in progressively reduced quantities, could be passed into the building. This extreme measure achieved the long desired result. On 1 September 1271, the cardinals appointed from their own number a commission of six to elect the Pope, and that same day, the six reached a decision. The man of their choice was

Teobaldo Visconti, the Archdeacon of Liege, who was neither cardinal, nor bishop, nor even yet a priest.

The interregnum, which had been of quite unprecedented duration, had lasted two years, nine months and three days, and is the longest on record. The next in length followed the death of Pope Nicholas IV (1288–1292), which lasted two years, three months and two days. The shortest conclave in the last three hundred years lasted less than twenty-four hours, during which Cardinal Eugenio Pacelli was elected Pope on the third ballot, in 1939, and took the name Pius XII. This was almost equalled in 1978, when Pope John Paul I (Cardinal Albino Luciani) was elected on the fourth ballot after thirty-six hours enclosure; alas, his pontificate lasted only thirty-three days. The shortest recorded reign was that of Pope Urban VII, which had a duration of a mere thirteen days; whereas Pope Pius IX's pontificate (1846–1878) lasted all of thirty-one years, seven months and twenty-three days, surpassing even St Peter himself.

The choice in 1271 was excellent, for Pope Gregory X is now numbered among the blessed in the Calendar of Saints. Profiting from the salutary lesson taught at Viterbo, this saintly, reforming pope decided that henceforward the 'conclave-system' was to be imposed on the cardinals as the normal manner in which they must elect a pope. It is interesting to note that the locking-up of the assembly in conclave was designed to keep the cardinals in, not to keep intruders out!

Where the conclave takes place

During the earliest centuries of the Church, the election of the Bishop of Rome – the Pope – was like that of any other residential bishop, in which the clergy and laity also participated. The earliest papal elections, therefore, were held in the Lateran Basilica, alongside which was the residence of the popes, the 'Vatican' of the Middle Ages. Two factors, however, contributed to change the pattern of papal elections.

Firstly, the lower clergy and the faithful gradually came to be excluded from the election, their participation being reduced to the acclamation of the new pope, while the actual business of electing him was reserved to the higher Roman clergy and principally to the cardinals. The appellation 'cardinal' comes from the Latin words '*cardo*' and '*cardine*', normally translated into English as 'hinge', or 'pivot'. This gives some idea of the importance of the functional roles played by these men in the life of the Christian community in Rome, which revolved around them in that they were the most trusted counsellors and ministers of the popes, forming a sort of senate. From as early as the twelfth century even distinguished prelates not resident in Rome were elevated to the cardinalate. The number of cardinals varied over the centuries. In

1587, Pope Sixtus V fixed the plenum of the College at seventy members; more recently, in 1973, Pope Paul VI modified this, raising the maximum number of electors to one hundred and twenty, thereby corresponding better to the present day requirements of a vastly expanding Church. *The Code of Canon Law* (Book II, Part II, Chapter III, Canons 349–359) provides a precise description of their function in the hierarchy of the Church today, with specific reference to the exclusive role of the Sacred College in the election of the Roman Pontiff.

Secondly, the widespread need for reform in the eleventh century forced the popes into undertaking long journeys, to hold diocesan synods and provincial councils throughout the length and breadth of Christendom. Frequently it happened that the Pope died away from Rome, when in some distant part of the Church. In this way necessity gave birth to the rule that the cardinals were to assemble as quickly as possible, and hold the papal election in the place where the previous pope had died. The election of Blessed Gregory X at Viterbo is an example of this custom. The rule was never changed, at least not explicitly, but the latest apostolic constitution now stipulates that the conclave will take place within the sovereign territory of Vatican City.

Since the election of Pope Martin V during the General Council at Constance in 1417, there has been only one papal election which did not take place in Rome. The sole exception is the conclave in which Pope Pius VII was elected. His predecessor, Pope Pius VI, had died at Valence, a prisoner of Napoleon Bonaparte, and it was only with the greatest difficulty that the cardinals – among them was the last of the Royal Stuarts, Prince Henry Benedict, the Cardinal Duke of York – convened at Venice in 1800, and held the conclave in the Benedictine monastery on the island of San Giorgio.

From the early fifteenth century until 1823, all the Roman conclaves were held in the Vatican, with only two exceptions, when the cardinals assembled instead in the Dominican convent, which adjoins the gothic church of S. Maria sopra Minerva, for the elections of Eugenius IV (1431) and Nicholas V (1447).

Pope Pius VII died in the Quirinal Palace, in 1823, and the cardinals decided to have the conclave there, where there was more suitable accommodation for them than at the Vatican. The conclaves continued to be held in the Quirinal, and it was there that Leo XII (1823), Pius VIII (1829), Gregory XVI (1831) and Pius IX (1846) were elected. During this pontificate, however, the troops of King Victor Emmanuel occupied the Papal States as part of the campaign for the unification of Italy, and in 1870, after a token resistance, the city of Rome fell into their hands. So 'Pio Nono' took refuge in the Vatican Palace where he remained until his death in 1878. All the popes since that time have been elected in the Vatican and Pope John Paul II's legislation makes it quite clear that for the future, papal elections will be held only within the independent territory of Vatican City State.

The Vatican

Certainly, the Vatican has much to recommend it as the place for electing the Roman Pontiff. Its historical associations cannot be equalled, and the same must be said for the splendour of the architectural setting. Situated between St Peter's Basilica and the papal residence is the Sistine Chapel, built by Pope Sixtus IV, from whom it takes its name, in 1475–83, to function as the principal chapel of the Vatican Palace. It is a plain, lofty, rectangular building, said to be modelled on Solomon's Temple in Jerusalem, about 40 metres in length, 13 in width, providing a floor area of approximately 520 square metres, and almost 21 in height (133 feet long, 45 feet wide, 65 feet high), lit by six large windows, situated high up on the walls of either side. The simplicity of design renders this chapel particularly suitable for the conclave, as it can be transformed easily into the election chamber, though stringent precautions must be taken to ensure that no audio-visual devices have been surreptitiously installed in the interior and adjacent area for recording the procedure, or transmitting information, in flagrant violation of the privacy demanded by the conclave.

The simplicity of the Sistine Chapel stops at the simplicity of its architectural design; the frescoes on its walls offer for the admiration of the world some of the the most sublime works of the masters of Italian Renaissance painting. The artists, who over a period of fifty years were commissioned to decorate the chapel, took for their theme the history of mankind, from the Creation of the world to the Last Judgment, through all its significant phases. The Creation, the Fall of Man, and the Flood sweep in glowing colours across the vaulting of the ceiling; the Deliverance of the Chosen People from captivity in Egypt occupies the left wall; the Redemption of mankind from sin, through the earthly life of Christ, occupies the right wall, and counterbalances the scenes of the Old Testament with scenes from the New Testament. On the end wall, behind the altar, forming a fabulous backdrop to this beautiful scheme of biblical scenes, rises Michelangelo's majestic fresco of the Last Judgment, portraying the inescapable destiny of Man.

It is against this significant setting that the drama of the papal election will be enacted. Sufficient desks and chairs, corresponding to the number of grand electors, are neatly arranged in several rows along each side of the chapel. A large table is positioned in the centre, before the altar, where the the ballots can be counted. The scene is set; we must now see who will be the actors.

Dramatis personae

Who are admitted to the conclave? In the first place, all the cardinals, including those whose names have only been officially published in consistory, even if they have not yet been formally inducted and sworn into the Sacred College, but with the exception of those who have attained their eightieth birthday (a provision introduced by Pope Paul VI in 1970) prior to the vacancy of the Apostolic See. Rather, the emphasis is on the obligation of each cardinal to attend the conclave, when summoned to the Vatican by the Cardinal Dean, unless some obviously grave reason beyond his control prevents him. There is a time limit of at least fifteen days in which to make the journey; when a maximum period of twenty days has elapsed, since the beginning of the interregnum, all the electors present must proceed to the election without further delay. If in fact a cardinal should arrive later, while the conclave is still in session, then he must be admitted to take part in the election at whatever stage it has reached.

The total number of electors may never exceed one hundred and twenty, which is considered sufficient to express the universality of the Church, since they were chosen specifically to represent as wide a spectrum as possible of its multiple culture and geographical extension. A remarkable transformation in the composition of the Sacred College has taken place in the

The Sistine Chapel prepared for the election.

course of this century, from being almost one hundred per cent European (and predominantly Italian) at the outset to a more balanced and proportional, even if not absolutely equitable, distribution, as it nears its close. Cardinals from Africa, North, Central and Latin America, Asia and Oceania now constitute more than half of the electoral body.

The right of admission is to be denied only to those who either refused to enter the conclave at the appointed time or left without sufficient reason and the consent of the majority of the electoral college. This must not be confused with the exceptional permission to leave the conclave, which may have to be granted on urgent medical grounds; when he has recuperated his health, the Cardinal may return and resume his place among the other electors.

After the cardinals comes a restricted group of officials and technicians, whose services are indispensable for the proper functioning of the conclave: the Secretary of the College of Cardinals, acting in the same role for the electoral assembly; the Master of Pontifical Liturgical Celebrations, with, in addition, two masters of ceremonies and two sacristans; an ecclesiastical assistant to the Cardinal Dean. There must also be available inside the area of the conclave a number of confessors to hear confessions in the different languages, two medical doctors for possible emergencies, together with adequate

The General Congregation of Cardinals.

and appropriate catering and domestic staff. If a cardinal elector requires a nurse in attendance, even during the period of the election, then suitable accommodation will be provided. All these persons must be approved by the Cardinal Camerlengo and his three cardinal assistants; prior to being admitted to the conclave, they must swear on oath to observe absolute secrecy, under pain of incurring the severest canonical penalties for any infringement, about anything they come to learn directly or indirectly regarding the election itself and to refrain from using audio or video equipment for purposes of recording these happenings.

The conclave opens

The conclave opens with great solemnity, its ceremonial conducted in meticulous observance of the protocol set out in the *Ordo Rituum Conclavis*, the order of rites to be performed in the course of the conclave. On the morning of the day appointed by the General Congregation, the cardinals celebrate in St Peter's Basilica a Votive Mass *Pro eligendo Papa*, to invoke the divine assistance of the Holy Spirit on the election of the Pope. In the early afternoon, the cardinal electors return to the Vatican and assemble in the Pauline Chapel, situated at the top of the *Scala Regia*, the grand staircase of the papal residence. Here the procession is formed for the entry into the conclave: vested in their scarlet robes, the cardinals make

The cardinals process from the Pauline Chapel.

their way to the Sistine Chapel to the accompaniment of the inspiring chant of the ninth century Latin hymn, *Veni, Creator Spiritus*, associated with many solemn acts of Catholic worship and familiar to us in the English translation 'Come, O Creator, Spirit blest/And in our souls take up thy rest'. They enter in order of seniority: first the Dean and cardinal bishops, followed by the cardinal priests and deacons, and in their wake comes the group of officials and assistants entrusted with specific duties and functions in strict connection with the conclave.

Having taken their places in the Chapel, the Cardinal Dean reads aloud to the cardinals the prescribed oath to observe faithfully and scrupulously the prescriptions contained in the Apostolic Constitution regarding the election of the Roman Pontiff and to maintain the strictest secrecy about all that occurs in the course of it. In due order, each elector takes the oath by repeating personally this short formula: 'And I, N. Cardinal N., do so promise, pledge and swear. So help me God and these Holy Gospels which I touch with my hand.'

When the last of the cardinal electors has taken the oath, the Master of Pontifical Liturgical Celebrations gives the order '*Extra omnes!*' – 'All out!' – and all unauthorised persons must leave the area of the conclave immediately. He himself remains behind, together with the specially designated orator, who has accepted the task

The cardinals at their places in the conclave.

of addressing the electoral college on the gravity of the duty incumbent on it and the paramount need for integrity of intention and wise discernment in choosing a new pope, with eyes fixed on God alone. After this they both leave the chapel. If there is nothing further to prevent the election from beginning, it may start immediately in accordance with the order and procedure stipulated in the papal decree.

Who are the Electors?

Who elects the Pope? After all that has been written, this question may appear unnecessary: obviously, the cardinals elect the Pope. The Apostolic Constitution states, in unequivocal terms, that the right to elect the Roman Pontiff belongs exclusively to the members of the College of Cardinals who have not yet celebrated their eightieth birthday at the time that the Holy See falls vacant. No exceptions whatsoever are made for ecclesiastics of any other grade; no sort of concessions to any secular power, or civil authority.

Even a General Council in session has no part in the election of a pope; with the death of the previous pope, the work of the Council is suspended automatically, no matter at what stage of the debates, while the Fathers must await its recall by the newly elected Pontiff, before they can continue their deliberations.

It is not unfitting, however, that the cardinals should be the electors; a glance back to the earliest centuries of the Church is sufficient to show that the papal election could not be in more rightful hands.

Our knowledge of the process of electing bishops in the early Church is very slight, but from authentic sources, such as the letter of St Clement of Rome to the Christian community at Corinth, written in the year 95 or 96, or the letters of St Cyprian, written many years later, around 251, we know that the election of a local bishop was a matter involving all members of the faithful. The bishops from the surrounding province, the local clergy and the laity met together in the cathedral, three days after the death of the previous bishop. There, in the cathedral, the election took place, and on the following Sunday the newly elected bishop received consecration from the hands of the other bishops of the province.

After the first General Council of the Church, held at Nicea, a town in Asia Minor, in the year 325, the emphasis was laid more on the part taken by the bishops and the higher clergy in the election; gradually the role of the lower clergy and the laity was reduced to one of mere acclamation of the newly-elect.

In Rome, this meant that the bishops from the dioceses around the City, together with the parish priests and the deacons, who were in charge of the seven regions into which the community was divided for administrative purposes, were the churchmen to whom the election of the new Bishop of Rome was always entrusted. Already the embryo of the College of Cardinals, structured internally into three grades of bishops, priests, and deacons, had clearly begun to emerge.

Cardinal bishops are still assigned nominally to the neighbouring 'suburbicarian dioceses' of Ostia, Albano, Frascati, Palestrina, Porto-Santa Ruffina, Sabina-Poggio Mirteo, and Velletri-Segni, though nowadays these highly populated sees are governed in reality by their respective active residential bishops in the normal way. This innovation was introduced by Pope John XXIII, in 1962, leaving the cardinal bishops with the mere title so as not to break the historical continuity.

Likewise, the ancient titular presbyteral churches and diaconal districts (and many more of recent creation) are assigned to the cardinal priests and deacons, thereby technically 'incardinating', or incorporating, them in the clergy of Rome, while allowing them to retain, at least for the majority of those not employed in the Roman Curia, their pastoral assignment as residential archbishops and bishops of dioceses scattered throughout the world.

A part in the election was also played either by the local aristocracy (on behalf of the Roman people) or by the Frankish and later by the German emperors, the political protectors of the Patrimony of St Peter, as the territory surrounding the City was then named. At times in the past, however, undue lay interference in the papal elections resulted in the intrusion of thoroughly unworthy candidates. In the span of years that separates the antipope Hippolytus (217–235) from the antipope Felix V (1439–1449), contested elections produced approximately thirty-six rival claimants to the papacy. Consequently emancipation of the ecclesiastical office from any secular authority became the predominant theme of a general reform of the Church in order to avert the recurrence of such scandals for the future.

A major step in that direction was taken in 1059, during a synod at the Lateran, when Pope Nicholas II (1059–1061) issued a formal decree establishing several prime factors of lasting canonical importance. Thenceforth the right to elect the Pope would pertain to the cardinals alone, among whom the cardinal bishops were given the decisive vote and the other cardinals only a consultative one. Though preferable, it was not necessary that the new pope be chosen from among the clergy of Rome, or that the election be held there, and from the moment of election, the newly-elect acquired full papal authority. It then remained for the rest of the clergy and the laity to be admitted, but simply to express their consent to the election.

Over a century later, in 1179, during the Third Lateran Council, Pope Alexander III (1159–1181) reaffirmed that the papal election was reserved exclusively to the cardinals, all of whom were to participate equally in the election with a decisive vote. Furthermore, he enacted that thenceforth a two-thirds majority of the Sacred College would be necessary for a valid election to preclude eventual contestation.

This was an instance of hindsight for at the time of his own election, in 1159, Cardinal Roland Bandinelli had been the candidate voted by the majority of the cardinals, while against him a minority of their colleagues set up an antipope styled Victor IV, who had three successors, thereby creating a schism in the Church that lasted all of seventeen years. Throughout this time the consecutive antipopes were aided and abetted by the German emperor, Frederick Barbarossa, who was in open conflict with Pope Alexander III over the independence of the Church from lay control in general and monarchical authority in particular. So restrictive measures, which may appear to have eroded the democratic process of electing the popes, were in fact adopted as means of defending the autonomy of the papacy from the interference of secular rulers in a struggle that endured over many centuries.

Undoubtedly, Archbishop Thomas Becket, assassinated in Canterbury Cathedral on 29 December 1170 by knights acting for King Henry II of England, was the most illustrious victim of that troubled era: little over two years later, on 21 February 1173, Pope Alexander III canonized him and down the centuries he has been venerated as a martyr for the liberty of the Church from external oppression.

The last attempt at political interference in the election of a pope occurred in 1903. During the conclave following the death of Pope Leo XIII, when the votes began to converge on Cardinal Mariano Rampolla del Tindaro, Cardinal Jan Puzyna, Archbishop of Cracow, acting on instructions from the Austrian Emperor Franz-Josef, registered a veto excluding this candidate. Evidently his imperial master judged the former Secretary of State as not sufficiently compliant towards the Hapsburgs and potentially over lenient towards French foreign policy. Rampolla was not elected. Less than six months later, however, the new pope, St Pius X (1903–1914) decreed (20 January 1904) an end forever to such meddling in the internal affairs of the Church.

Any alternative?

And so the election of the Pope has remained exclusively in the hands of the cardinals down to the present day, including the modifications introduced by Pope Paul VI in 1965, when he admitted to the ranks of the Sacred College, immediately after the cardinal bishops, certain Patriarchs of the Eastern Churches in communion with the Apostolic See; and also when, in 1970, he exonerated

the very elderly cardinals from the stress and
inconvenience hitherto associated with the conclaves.

No one claims that this is the perfect method for
choosing a pope, as the election of 'bad popes' in the past
only too clearly proved. Since the days of the Second
Vatican Council (1962–1965), with the greater emphasis
on collegiality in the life of the Church, considerable
attention has been given to the question of finding a valid
alternative to the present system, one that would extend
beyond the cardinals and associate other members of the
episcopate (and even of the laity) in the electoral act.
Some suggestions are quite unrealistic; others would only
pose problems of a different kind. The members of the
Synod of Bishops currently in office might guarantee a
better representation of the local churches and a future
trend may move in that direction, but, for the present, the
form of the papal election remains substantially
unchanged, except for those minor modifications which
have been deemed opportune and timely.

Who may be elected?

Is the choice of the cardinals in any way limited? Strictly
speaking they are at liberty to elect any male Christian,
cleric or layman, who is not a heretic, or in schism, or
notorious for simony, and has reached the age of reason.

The last person to be elected Pope who was not a
cardinal at the time of his election was an archbishop of

Bari, Bartolomeo Prignano. He was elected to the papacy on 8 April 1378 and took the name of Pope Urban VI. It is a name which history has never forgotten, because with his election the Church was plunged into that dreadful period, which lasted for forty years, known as the Great Schism of the West. The cardinals averred that the local mob had interfered in the conclave, that they had acted under duress and the election was thereby rendered invalid, and so they proceeded to hold another conclave and elected a second pope. Ordinary Catholics were confused to see two, and later even three different popes, all claiming their allegiance. Consequently, since the fourteenth century no person has been elected Pope who was not a member of the College of Cardinals at the time.

Therefore, while (the Servant of God) Abbot Columba Marmion, or Brother (now Blessed) Edmund Ignatius Rice, or even the writer Gilbert Keith Chesterton (whom Pope Pius XI termed 'a devoted son of Holy Church and gifted defender of the Catholic Faith') were not explicitly excluded, there does not seem much possibility, or expediency, of the cardinals electing someone, who is not already one of their own number.

Certainly, in making his choice a cardinal elector must not allow himself to be guided by merely human considerations, such as personal friendship, or aversion for any particular person, or to be influenced by force, or fear, or the suggestions of the mass media. The glory of

God and the good of souls should inspire his judgment, so that his vote is given for the person, even outside the electoral college, whom he considers most suited and qualified to govern the Universal Church.

Election procedure

How must the cardinals elect a new pope? Pope John Paul II has decreed that the only form is by secret ballot – *per scrutinium* – and that a majority of two thirds of the votes of the electors present is necessary for the valid election of the Roman Pontiff. But what if a cardinal votes for himself? The eventuality is no longer considered to invalidate an essential quorum. Only when the total number of votes is not divisible into three equal parts will one additional vote be required for validity.

This has been the normal form of election by which the popes of the last eight, or nine hundred years have been chosen, and it is necessary to devote more time to an examination of this method, in which each step will be briefly, but clearly, explained. The whole process can be divided into three simple phases: the preparation for the ballot; the secret ballot itself; the counting of the votes and checking of the results. We shall examine each part separately.

Having taken their places in the Sistine Chapel, but before the cardinal electors proceed to the secret ballot proper, some preliminary formalities must first be completed. The names of nine cardinals are extracted at random by the most junior of the cardinal deacons: they are to serve as 'scrutineers', 'infirmarians', and 'revisers', whose special functions will be explained shortly, at the proper time. Meantime the masters of ceremonies will have distributed at least two or three voting forms to each elector, after which the Secretary of the Conclave, the Master of Pontifical Liturgical Celebrations and his assistants must all withdraw from the Sistine Chapel and the door is closed behind them by the junior cardinal deacon, so that the cardinals are left entirely on their own during the time when they fill in their ballot forms, cast them, and announce the number recorded for each person. It would be difficult to overstress the secrecy that surrounds the actual election of a new pope!

Secret Ballot

On the desk before him each cardinal has the simple ballot form, rectangular in shape, on which is printed, in Latin, the words:

Eligo in Summum Pontificem

N. N.

That is, 'I elect as Supreme Pontiff, N. N.' The electors write in the vacant lower space the name of him for whom they wish to cast their vote. As far as possible, they should try to alter their normal handwriting so that it is not easily recognisable as theirs. Having completed a ballot form, each cardinal must fold it lengthwise and in such a way that the name of his choice cannot be seen. The completed form should appear so:

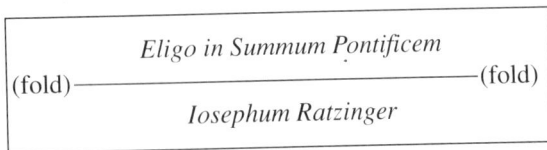

Eligo in Summum Pontificem

(fold) ——————————————————————— (fold)

Iosephum Ratzinger

This is the first phase of the secret ballot. The second phase – the *scrutinium* proper – follows immediately.

Having completed and folded his ballot form, each cardinal takes it between the thumb and index finger of his right hand, and, holding the form aloft, he approaches the altar, according to rank. A very large chalice, covered with a paten, has been placed in readiness to receive the ballot forms. Standing before the altar, the cardinal pronounces in a clear and audible voice the following oath:

'I call as my witness Christ the Lord, who will be my judge, that my vote is given to the one whom, before God, I think should be elected.'

Having taken this oath in the presence of his colleagues, the cardinal places the ballot form on the paten and, tilting the paten, lets the form slide into the chalice. With that, he bows in reverence to the altar, and returns to his place. If any of the cardinal electors present for the secret ballot is unable to go to the altar, because of some disability, then the third scrutineer goes to him: the infirm elector, having pronounced the prescribed oath, hands his folded form to the scrutineer, who brings it in full view of the others to the altar, places it on the paten and slides it into the chalice in the approved manner.

What about sick cardinals who cannot come to the Sistine Chapel to cast their votes, but are confined to their apartments in the residential hospice? This is where the three cardinal infirmarians come in. Their duty is to go to the sick cardinals, so that even these electors may record their votes. For this purpose there is a special box with a slit at the top, through which a folded ballot form can be dropped into the box. First the cardinal scrutineers show the open box to the other electors to verify that it is completely empty; the box is then locked and the key deposited on the altar. The cardinal infirmarians take the box and a sufficient number of ballot forms on a small tray to each sick cardinal, who casts his vote in the normal way, the oath being taken in the presence of the three deputed cardinals. Having completed their mission, they return the locked box to the cardinal scrutineers, who open it and ascertain that the number of forms corresponds exactly to the number of sick electors, placing them singly on the paten and sliding them all together into the chalice. The three infirmarians may perform this duty while the process of voting is in progress, having first cast their own votes immediately after the senior cardinal elector.

Counting the Votes

When all the cardinals have voted, the three scrutineers come forward to count the votes. The first scrutineer shakes up the ballot forms in the chalice several times in order to mix them; the third scrutineer takes each form separately from the large chalice, and transfers them one by one to a second chalice, which is empty and ready to receive them. If it should happen that the number of ballot papers does not correspond with the number of electors, in that case the ballot is null and has to be ignored. These ballot papers will be burned and the process of voting must be repeated. On the other hand, when the number of forms does tally with the number of electors, then the three scrutineers seat themselves at the table and begin to unfold the votes and announce the result of the voting in the following way.

The first scrutineer takes a form, opens it, silently reads and makes a note of the name written on it, and hands it to the second scrutineer. The second scrutineer does likewise, passing the opened form to the third scrutineer, who, having read the name, declares it in a clear voice to the electoral college and records the name written on the ballot. The scrutineers continue until the last ballot form has been announced, while the cardinals note the results on pieces of paper prepared for that purpose. At the conclusion the scrutineers announce the total number of votes obtained by each individual and write the different names on a separate sheet of paper.

During the opening of the ballots should the scrutineers discover two ballot forms folded in such a way that they appear to have been completed and cast by one elector, if they contain the same name they count as one vote; if they express two different names, both votes will be discounted, but in neither case is the voting session annulled.

This is the crucial moment of the balloting. If anyone has received two-thirds of the votes cast, then he has been canonically elected Pope. Only when the total number of the ballots cast is not divisible by three is it required that the candidate be elected by a majority of two-thirds plus one.

Having announced the result of the voting, the third scrutineer takes the ballots and threads them all together, inserting the needle through the first word '*Eligo*' of the formula printed on each form, so that there is less risk of them being dispersed. A knot is tied at each end of the thread to secure them and the bundle of votes is carefully put to one side.

The third and final phase of the secret ballot now takes place. In order to ensure the accuracy and veracity of the count, the voting forms and records of the ballot are examined by the three cardinal revisers, and when they are satisfied that the counting has been performed accurately, the ballot forms and notes are taken to be burned in a specially installed stove, the brainwave of a master of ceremonies in the mid-eighteenth century, the better to dispel the smoke from the chamber. This must be done by the three scrutineers, before the cardinals leave the Sistine Chapel, with the help of the Secretary of the Conclave and the masters of ceremonies, who have been readmitted to the chamber at this stage by the junior cardinal deacon.

When the ballot has been conclusive and the new Pope is elected, the ballot forms and records are burned alone in the stove and a thin curl of white smoke rises from the tall metal chimney, erected against the gable-end of the Sistine Chapel. This is the sign eagerly awaited by the world; the sign that the cardinals in conclave have accomplished their task, that the interregnum is at an end. On the other hand, if the voting has been inconclusive and has not yet resulted in a valid election, all the papers are burned along with some chemical substance which will emit dense black smoke, easily visible in St Peter's Square. In this way the result of the balloting is made known to the crowds, waiting expectantly for the signal from the conclave. In the past it also gave the cue to the guard at the fortress of Castel Sant'Angelo to fire a salvo from the cannon and alert the populace of Rome that the new Pope was about to be proclaimed.

Should the election begin on the afternoon of the entry of the cardinals into the conclave, only one ballot is to be held. If no one is elected on that first day, then, on the following days, both in the morning and in the afternoon, after a further inconclusive ballot, the electors shall proceed immediately to a second vote. All the formalities of the ceremonial contained in the order of service for the conclave are to be diligently observed, without, however, repeating the oath, or choosing new scrutineers, infirmarians, and revisers for the second round.

Impasse

After balloting has been carried out in the prescribed way for three days without resulting in an election, voting is to be suspended at most for a day to allow a pause for prayer and informal discussion among the cardinals. Balloting will take place each day, twice in the morning, and again twice in the afternoon [72-73]. After balloting has been carried out as prescribed for three days without arriving at the conclusive result, the process will be suspended for one day, before being resumed in the usual manner. Another pause may be needed after seven more ballots, and again after another seven ballots [74]. Faced with this impasse, calculated at around 33/34 ballotings, the Camerlengo will ask the Electors for their opinion on how to proceed and the election will proceed in accordance with what the absolute majority decides. For the validity of the election, however, a two thirds majority of votes will always be required, even in the extreme case of voting only on the two *Papabili* who obtained the greatest suffrage in the immediately preceding ballot, and are excluded themselves from voting in the resumed round of balloting (cf. *Motu Proprio* of Benedict XVI, 11th June 2007, abrogating the provision contained in paragraph 75 of the Apostolic Constitution *Universi Dominici Gregis* that made a simple majority of votes sufficient for a valid election in these unusual circumstances).

In the past, some conclaves were prolonged for many months, even for years, but recent conclaves have all been of short duration. The latest changes in the composition of the electoral college, especially the increase in the number of electors to one hundred and twenty and the greater internationalization of the participants, with all the cultural and language barriers which that implies, may make it more difficult for the cardinals to reach a rapid conclusion. A larger group normally takes longer to decide than a smaller group: communication and agreement were easier a century ago, when the vast majority were European in origin and predominantly Italian by birth. Although the whole world is watching and waiting for the outcome of the papal election, the cardinals need not feel under pressure to act hastily, unlike in previous conclaves when very elderly and often infirm men were admitted to vote and the accommodation was spartan and inadequate.

Of less importance by far is the elimination from the Apostolic Constitution of alternative modes of election. One form was called '*per inspirationem*' – 'by inspiration', when in conclave the cardinals acclaimed unanimously and unequivocally expressed the person whom thereby they elected Pontiff, though without any formal ballot. The last recorded example took place in 1621 at the election of Cardinal Alessandro Ludovisi, who reigned as Pope Gregory XV (died 8 July 1623). The other method was '*per compromissum*' – 'by compromise' or agreement given under oath by all the electors in conclave to accept as canonically elected the nominee chosen by a select committee composed of three, five or seven cardinals, and abide by that choice. The election of Pope Gregory X at Viterbo in 1271 was obtained in this way. Both modes are abolished and henceforth the only form of electing the Pope is by secret ballot.

Acceptance

When the election has taken place and its validity recognized, the junior cardinal deacon summons the Secretary of the Conclave and the Master of Pontifical

Liturgical Celebrations to the chamber. The Cardinal Dean, in the name of the whole college of electors, asks the assent of the newly elected in the following way:

'Do you accept your canonical election as Supreme Pontiff?'

Whoever he may be must not shrink from taking on the onerous duties of such a high office; humbly, he should submit to the divine Will, clearly manifested by the votes of the electors. In imposing the burden, God assuredly will give him the strength to shoulder its weight and accomplish the office with the help of His grace. At the very moment of giving an affirmative answer, accepting the election, but provided he is already sacramentally ordained to the hierarchical rank of the episcopate, the person elected immediately becomes the Bishop of Rome, true Pope and Head of the College of Bishops, and acquires full and absolute authority over the Church.

The Cardinal Dean addresses a second question to the new Pope:

'By what name do you wish to be called?'

The Holy Father, following an agelong custom, announces the name that he wishes to bear during his pontificate. The first newly elected pope to change his name was Mercurius, who preferred (for fairly obvious reasons – Mercury was a pagan god) to style himself Pope John II (533–535). He was imitated in this by some of his successors, but it is only with Pope Sylvester II (999–1003) that the practice really becomes traditional. In the course of the centuries since his time, only three cardinals have opted to retain their baptismal names: after the conclave Giuliano della Rovere styled himself Pope Julius II (1503–1513), which was not much of a change from his original name of Julian; his example was followed by Adrian Florensz (a Dutchman by birth and the last non-Italian to be elected, until the election of Karol Wojtyla in 1978) and Marcello Cervini, both of whom reigned for exceptionally brief pontificates as Pope Adrian VI (1522–1523), and Pope Marcellus II (1555).

The practice did not originate with St Peter, as some people imagine. It was our Blessed Lord Himself who imposed a new name on the fisherman of Galilee: 'You are Simon, son of John; you are to be called "*Cephas*" – meaning "Rock"' (*Jn* 1, 42). In Aramaic '*kepha*' means 'rock', the equivalent of '*petros*' in Greek. It was a prophetic nickname.

Motives of the most varied kind have inspired the popes in their choice. In the age of the Renaissance, Pope Pius II (1458–1464), formerly Aeneas Sylvius Piccolomini, recounts in his personal *Commentaries* that he chose this name in allusion to '*pius Aeneas*' of Virgil's epic poem '*Aeneid*'. In 1503 Cardinal Francesco Piccolomini, a nephew of Pius II, also chose this name in deference to his late uncle, but reigned as Pope Pius III for only twenty-six days. In modern times, Cardinal Giacomo della Chiesa, archbishop of Bologna prior to election, styled himself Pope Benedict XV (1914–1922), precisely because a predecessor as archbishop, Cardinal Prospero Lambertini, had preceded him in the papacy as Pope Benedict XIV (1740–1758). Pope John XXIII (1958–1963) took that name simply because his father's name was Giovanni, or John. And Pope John Paul II chose this title out of respect for his immediate predecessor Pope John Paul I (1978), whose pontificate lasted only thirty-three days. In almost two thousand years, however, no one has dared to be called 'Peter'; in 983, the newly elected Pope, whose baptismal name was Pietro, styled himself John XIV (983–984), rather than be acclaimed as Peter II. And John is the name that has most frequently been chosen after election to the papacy.

The Master of Pontifical Liturgical Celebrations, acting as notary and having as witnesses his two assistants, draws up a document testifying to the acceptance of the election and the Pontiff's choice of name.

If the new Pope is not already a bishop, he must be ordained to the episcopate immediately by the Cardinal Dean, in accordance with liturgical usage, before homage is paid to him by the electors, or the result of the election and his proclamation are made known to the world. The last time this happened was at the election of Cardinal

Mauro Alberto Cappellari, on 2 February 1831; hitherto he was only a Camaldolese abbot and was consecrated Bishop and crowned as Pope Gregory XVI four days later.

The new Pope is led to a small robing-room adjacent to the Sistine Chapel, where all during the conclave the appropriate robes have been laid out in readiness for the happy outcome of the election. White silk soutanes of three different sizes, large, medium and small, are prepared, so that he can change into the papal soutane which fits him best. He puts on the white silk sash, the lace rochet, the red slippers, the scarlet shoulder cape, the richly embroidered stole and the white zucchetto, or skull-cap.

Returning to the Sistine Chapel, the Pope seats himself on a faldstool placed before the altar and receives the first homage of the cardinal electors, who come one by one in order of seniority. The Camerlengo slips the gold Fisherman's Ring, symbolic of the newly assumed office, onto his finger, which the Pontiff returns to him immediately, so that the self-imposed pontifical name can be engraved around the rim. The first act of homage and obedience concludes with the singing of the *Te Deum*, a Latin anthem that dates from the fifth century expressing jubilation and gratitude to almighty God for His manifold gifts, the equivalent of the English hymn 'Praise we now the Lord our God, all mankind in chorus'.

Proclamation

Outside in St Peter's Square, hundreds of thousands of excited people have transferred their gaze from the Sistine Chapel, where, a half hour or so before, the wisp of white smoke – the *fumata* – told of a decisive ballot, and they have turned their attention, instead, to the great central balcony of the Basilica. At any moment, the senior cardinal deacon will come to announce to the crowded Square, and to the whole world, the choice made by the cardinal electors during the conclave. This proclamation is made with the Latin formula: '*Annuntio vobis gaudium magnum; habemus Papam! [Eminentissimum ac Reverendissimum Dominum, Dominum] N. [Cardinalem] N., qui sibi nomen imposuit N.*', which means: 'I announce a great joy to you; we have a pope! The [most Eminent and] most Reverend Lord N. [Cardinal] N. who has taken the name N.' In this way, the baptismal names and the surname of the new Pope, together with the name he has chosen for himself, are made known to the public. Immediately thereafter, the Holy Father himself comes to the central loggia of St Peter's and imparts his first Apostolic Blessing *Urbi et Orbi* – to the City of Rome and to the World. The conclave is over; the Holy See is no longer vacant; another pontificate has already begun.

The new Pope appears on the central balcony.

Chief Shepherd of the Flock

Within a short period after the election, the Sacred College
of Cardinals will form a crown around the new Pope and
present him to the Universal Church as Chief Shepherd in
a solemn liturgical rite of inauguration, culminating in the
placing of the Pallium, – a specially modelled narrow stole
of white wool embroidered with six black silk crosses, –
around his shoulders; three jewelled gold pins hold it in
place on the Pope's breast and back, and on his left
shoulder. It dates from very early times and was worn as a
scarf, being originally of much more ample proportions; in
the course of centuries it was reduced in size to its present
dimension and form and became the symbol of the
plenitude of episcopal jurisdiction, which consequently
has restricted its use, since 1978, to only a privileged few,
namely to the Pope himself, to metropolitan archbishops
and the Latin Patriarch of Jerusalem. The senior cardinal
deacon performs the ceremony of investiture, pronouncing
in Latin the following formula:

> Blessed be God, Who has chosen you as Shepherd of
> the Universal Church, entrusting you with this apostolic
> ministry. May you shine brilliantly during long years of
> earthly life, until, when called by our Lord, you are
> vested with immortality as you enter his celestial
> kingdom. Amen.

The cardinals all come forward one by one in order of seniority and repeat their homage to the new Roman Pontiff in an exchange of the Kiss of Peace. The liturgy continues with the Eucharistic Sacrifice of Mass, presided over by His Holiness as principal celebrant, now at the apex of his role in the Church, the focal point of that converging communion of love which unites all the faithful into one mystical body in Christ. At the conclusion of these sacred rites the Holy Father once more solemnly bestows his Apostolic Blessing *Urbi et Orbi*, to the Eternal City and to the wide World.

Prayers for the Pope from the Roman Missal

For the Election of a Pope

Lord God, you are our eternal shepherd and guide. In your mercy grant your Church a shepherd who will walk in your ways and whose watchful care will bring us your blessing.

We ask this through our Lord Jesus Christ, your Son, who lives and reigns with you and the Holy Spirit, one God, for ever and ever. Amen.

For the Pope
(especially on the anniversary of election)

Father of providence, look with love on N. our Pope, your appointed successor to Saint Peter on whom you built your Church. May he be the visible centre and foundation of our unity in faith and love.

Grant this through our Lord Jesus Christ, your Son, who lives and reigns with you and the Holy Spirit, one God, for ever and ever. Amen.

God our Father, shepherd and guide, look with love on N. your servant, the pastor of your Church. May his word and example inspire and guide the Church, and may he, and all those entrusted to his care, come to the joy of everlasting life.

Grant this through our Lord Jesus Christ, your Son, who lives and reigns with you and the Holy Spirit, one God, for ever and ever. Amen.

Lord, source of eternal life and truth, give to your shepherd N. a spirit of courage and right judgment, a spirit of knowledge and love. By governing with fidelity those entrusted to his care may he, as successor to the apostle Peter and vicar of Christ, build your Church into a sacrament of unity, love, and peace for all the world.

We ask this through our Lord Jesus Christ, your Son, who lives and reigns with you and the Holy Spirit, one God, for ever and ever. Amen.